Lola E. Peters

Copyright © 2013 Lola E. Peters

Poetry

ISBN 978-0-9898658-0-7

All rights reserved. Written permission must be secured from the author to use or reproduce any text in this book, in print or electronic format, except for brief quotation in reviews or articles. For permission, contact the author at lola.e.peters@gmail.com

Cover photography, book cover and layout by Lola E. Peters

Acknowledgements

This collection of poems would not be possible without my bestie Nita Penfold, who has encouraged my writing and goaded me to bring it to the public. Blame her!

Thanks also to Seattle's *African American Writers' Alliance* for their continued encouragement and support; the good folks at Shunpike (www.shunpike.org) for supporting the dream that has become *Poetry+Motion*; Niela Miller and Janette Brown for helping me find the unseen bridges; and my friends and family for their feedback, wisdom, and insight.

Table of Contents

Songs From Undead Poets vi

Politics

The Hero Speaks 2
Afghanistan. 4
The Great American Traitor 5
Free Admission. 6
Repatriation: What if it was me? 8
Bi- Yourself 10
A Toast 11
Legacy 13
Legacy of a Man 14
Prisoners of War 15

Religion

Evolution 18
Messiah 19
My Space 20
My Heaven 21
The Woman's Prayer 22
American Ethic 23
View From the Sky Box 24
View From the Sky Box 26
Grandma Lucy (Dinknesh) 27
Telescope Woman 28
God's Man 29
Religious.
Right. 30
Yom Kippur 31
Grace 32
2:00am 33
11 34
Eternal Life 35
Endings 36

Table of Contents
(continued)

Not intended for polite company

Daniel's Song 38
That Finger 39
Barbie Dogs. 40
The Fox 41
White Widow Spider 42
When Bills Come Due 43
Crystal 44
Who are you? 45
Gold chains 46
The Soloist. 47
Forty-three 48
Remember Time. 49
Dreamer. 50
Mrs. B, It's About Your Son 51
Poetry 101 52
The end 53

Songs From Undead Poets
(based on the painting by Rajaa Gharbi)

We bring waters
Dug from the deep aquifers
Of our experience and memory
To nourish and strengthen you
Amidst torments and fears
And refresh you in times of peace
So we may all enjoy
The beauty of your soul in bloom.
Drink deep.

Politics

The Hero Speaks

I lie here night after night
Riddled with guilt
Gulping down rage
Shaking with secret shame
Wanting to reach beyond this eternal barrier

To tell you that I am just a man who:
was leaving tomorrow on vacation
was in love with my wife
needed to get my tires rotated
just filed for divorce to marry my assistant
forgot to pick up my clothes from the cleaners
cheated on my taxes
loved my kids
hoped to close another deal today
stole from my company
was writing the novel that no one wanted to publish
hated my job
loved my job
loved my boyfriend more than my family
loved my family more than my girlfriend
hated war
wanted to kill
didn't want to die

To tell you that I am just a woman who:
forgot to eat breakfast this morning
just started menopause
didn't want this child just discovered in my belly
had a migraine
yelled at my kids
baked fresh cookies for my staff meeting
drank too much
was in debt over my head
was closing on a new home today
loved to dance in the nude
had a secret second job
was going on my first date tonight
loved living alone
hated living alone
was about to celebrate 25 years in a loveless marriage
just met the love of my life

But you have covered my mouth
With crime tape
Marked "HERO"
So my true story can never be told
And the depth of my humanity never exposed
Setting aspirations for others that can never be met
Using a single action to trap me in your mythology
Like a butterfly encased at the height of its beauty
Keeping me from my full humanity
Burying me under the weight of your fantasies
Until no one truly knows me
As anything other than a statistic.

Afghanistan

I wish someone would just
Come out and tell
The good people of Afghanistan
How this works.

First we hate you,
Label you with every awful name
We can conceive of
Killer, monster, commie; and our new favorite,
Terrorist.

We fight a bit
Always making sure
That our prominent people
And their families
Are safely tucked away
And can come to no harm.

Then we take money
From our children's education
From the hospitals that care for our elders
From our music, dance, poetry and art
And give it to your dictators
In bucketloads

Until eventually
Your country starts to grow
Even thrive
Rebuilding itself
While ours decays

Look it up
Japan, Germany, Vietnam, Russia.
This is how we "help."

Somebody
Please
Tell the good people of Afghanistan.
Just don't tell
The people of the United States.

The Great American Traitor

A $14-million bonus in 2008,
Just like the one he got the year before
And would get the year after.

Every dollar had the fingerprint
Of a $9-an-hour clerk
Who stood for eight hours
Knowing she or he would keep only pennies from each sale.
Every day
Smiling to condescending customers
Convincing them to buy
Yet one more thing they have no need of

In 2008 he laid off 750 workers in Seattle.
The next year
He expanded that to nearly 10,000 nationwide
Chicago, St. Louis, Miami, San Francisco.

And now
His political party
Calls him a "job creator"
And wants to give him
The pennies left in the pockets
Of those he made jobless, homeless, hungry, scared.

I call him the Great American Traitor
With no care for his fellow citizens
No care for his nation
Care only for his own acquisitive greed.
Willing to sacrifice everyone
So that he can sit atop the mountain of worthless paper
And beat his hairless chest.

Free Admission

I reached my arms toward you
Oh land of shining seas
My dreams locked in tight bundles
My hope: you held the keys.

In one box was my knowledge
From ancient schools and new
Another held the skills I learned
To think, to make, to do.

Wrapped tight and close against my heart
The bundle treasured dear
The wisdom of my ancestors
Their voices proud and clear.

I stepped onto this treasured land
Joy bubbled from my soul
Awaiting that magic moment
When I'd be myself; whole.

And then began your sorting:
One label on my skin
Another on my gender
Yet more set deep within.

You've stripped me of my language,
My garb you ripped to shreds
Sometimes it almost felt as if
You really wished me dead.

You've moved me to the outside
Then chased me to the edge
Each time I find my way back
Your fear finds a new wedge.

It's not your love I ask for
It's not your soul I seek
Just one small chance to be myself
And climb internal peaks

I'll give you all the credit
And benefits accrued
For just the opportunity
To be fully understood

So here I stand United States
My arms outstretched to you
To ask you one more time
What are you going to do?

Repatriation: What if it was me?
for Palestine

I dreamed of a house with arched doorways
With a steel front door painted a dark burnt orange
Walking from the backyard with fresh grilled vegetables
Picked from the earth beneath my feet
Through the side yard
Up the stone front steps
Through the unlocked door.

The rumors were true
We had 48 hours to pack only what we treasured
From all the generations of our family core
And be gone.

Some struggled, fought; died.
The world declared it must be so.
Reparations.
Land in exchange for silence.

The National Guard came for us.
In their armed convoys we traveled westward across the border,
The baby crying our inconsolable heartache the whole way.

Tents met us.
Tents.
As far as the eye could see.
Tents.
Three, four, five families, strangers, to a tent.

Ten years they've promised us better conditions
But there is no money
Some, those with family elsewhere
Or secreted stashes
Or insider knowledge
Or collaborators' hearts
Have moved on to new places.

Me?
I long to shake this Eastern Washington dust from my feet
And feel the cool, fresh air of my Montana mountain home again.

I dreamed of a house with arched doorways
With a steel front door painted a dark burnt orange
Walking from the backyard with fresh grilled vegetables
Picked from the earth beneath my feet
Through the side yard
Up the stone front steps
Though the unlocked door.

Bi- Yourself

They all want me to be bi-racial
Not White
'Cause clearly this honey-tone is tinged with the sun's kiss
    on a southern continent.
Not Black
'Cause I don't speak words laced with the undulating rhythms
    of the Africa in their imaginations
Not White
'Cause I *do* have an attitude
Not Black
'Cause I'm intellectually controlled by gears
    they think I can't drive.

Oh, it would be easier
To be bi-racial
To forget ten years of my suburban California childhood
    laced with "hey nigger"
To wash away the stains of white men's presumptions
    about my body.
To erase the pain on my father's face
        when his long-distance employers realized
        their top salesman was Black
        and took away his awards
To brush off the jobs, promotions, opportunities
        given to people less knowledgeable or skilled
        than me

But take those away and I don't exist.
They are my soul's posts and beams.
African born, American made
So True Black inside
That it bleeds through my yellow skin
And challenges everyone's presumptions.

Apparently,
Only I am not confused
About my identity.

A Toast
November 4, 2008

To our parents and grandparents
Whose stubbornness and passion
Cracked open doors where there were walls
So that we could see the light.

To their parents and all who came before
Who made a way out of no way
And held us together with faith, wisdom and love
Even as we were separated.

To those among us
Who have been "the first" or "the only"
Yet wake up each morning and go
To hold the door frame in place for the next one.

To our children and grandchildren
Who live in the light of our projected vision
And illuminate our lives
With their unencumbered joy.

And most of all
To the community organizers
Who never stop believing in us
And give their lives to us with unconditional love.

We are not done,
But today we raise our hearts in gratitude
And rededicate ourselves.
To justice, equality, and integrity.

Keep hope alive!
Sí, se puede.
Viva!

China Pattern

She hovered over each pattern of China
Thoughtless of the maker's touch
And heedless of his children's hunger
Careless of his Muse's yearning
Eager only to quell her impulse to own
Unaware of the psychic transfer
That obligated her to the world beyond
Her Self.

Legacy

There are moments
when the sweet silence
of the abyss
beckons with arms outstreched
whispering
promises of peace.

Then
Harriet,
  or Martin
    or Langston
      or Zora
        or Dolly
          or Roberto

or   or   or

calls out to me:
"Where you goin', girl?
We got work to do."

And I remember
Peace without Justice
is Tyranny.

Legacy of a Man
for George 43

He thinks he's a man
All dressed up in daddy's clothes
Wearing daddy's guns
Hangin' with daddy's pals.

But a real man
   Knows how to listen
   Long enough to hear the resonance of truth.
And a real man
   Can separate his needs
   From the needs of the world
It's a real man
   Who sees his own strength mirrored
   In the eyes of strong women
A real man
   Aches with the violence that is proof
   Of his failure to find the care-full path
A real man's
   Actions reflect the impact of other men's grief
   And every mother's tears.

No.
He's just a boy
Playing with daddy's toys
Tripping over thoughts too big for his uncurious mind
Too inexperienced to realize he has lost the real war
For his soul.

Prisoners of War

Fighting,   Mama
Fleeing,   Daddy
Struggling.   Baby girl
                   Son
Chained,   Grandmamma
Dragged,   Papa
Transported.   Uncle
                   Auntie
Starving   Sister
Working.   Brother
Dying.   Ten Generations

Working   Foreign bellies filled
 Dying   By your hands
  Working   Foreign soil
  Dying   Shoveled on your bones
Working   Foreign hands
 Dreaming   Pick your daisies
  Dying.   Skyscrapers become
Dreaming   Your headstones
 Hoping
Working   And The Man
                   and his Woman
Dying   say they owe you no apology,
                   your children no recompense.

    it's the debt-free american dream

Religion

Evolution

The ape knows:
It's the meat of the fruit
That sustains and refreshes.

But you,
Oh cultured Man,
Discard the fruit
After tasting the peel
Then wonder
Why you're not
Satisfied.

Messiah

One by One
They touch your hem.
"Heal me, feed me,
Make me special"
They plead.

I stand to the side,
Confident of my wholeness
Able to feed myself,
Secure in my uniqueness.
"Come, friend,
Walk the beach with me"
I ask.

You are lifted by the multitude,
Carried by wave after needy wave.
I walk the shore at night
Alone
Waiting for the tide to turn.

My Space

Where is the holy place?
The place where brown-skinned people can stand tall
Without huddling
Where black-skinned people can speak Truth
Without whispering
Where tears flow from tenderness
And not rage
Where all that's seen can be told
Without fear
Where laughing eyes belong to adults
As well as children
Where a gentle spirit
Can find peace?
Where is that holy place?
When I find it, it will be my space.

My Heaven

In an open field
Hedged by California golden poppies
And knee-high dahlias,
Microphone in hand,
Twirling like Julie Andrews' Maria,
Belting a tune from the toes up,
While Joe Sample runs those beautiful, sinuous fingers
Up the ebony and down the ivory
And 'Trane blows blue
Waves of peace around the globe.

The Woman's Prayer

There is a dream I cannot face.
Its shadows interrupt my daily trudge.
Lillith's[1] demons call me out to play.

Oh, Lillith; goddess of the wild,
Queen of the night:
Hair of dancing fire; Eyes of iridescent emeralds
Fire on fire, light of light
Free, Seducer, Siren, Temptress.
Joy of Life
Magician, Trickster, Doubter.

Your daughter/servant/sister begs your mercy.

Let me live in peace
Among the daughters of Eve
...And the sons of Adam.

[1] *In Jewish folklore, from the 8th–10th centuries onwards, Lilith is depicted as Adam's first wife, who was created at the same time and from the same earth as Adam. This contrasts with Eve, who was created from one of Adam's ribs. The legend was greatly developed during the Middle Ages. In the 13th Century writings of Rabbi Isaac ben Jacob ha-Cohen, for example, Lilith left Adam after she refused to become subservient to him and then would not return to the Garden of Eden after she mated with archangel Samael. The resulting Lilith legend is still commonly used as source material in modern Western culture, literature, occultism, fantasy, and horror.*

American Ethic

On this below-freezing
Winter's night
Mary, Joe & baby Jes
Huddle between cardboard walls
Under the Spokane Street overpass
While all of America kneels to pray
For Britney's success in rehab.

View From the Sky Box

The women represented every corner of earth.
After a week of committees, panels and seminars
They decided.
It was time for "the question",
So they asked the Council of Archangels
For a meeting with The Almighty.

"What" asked The Almighty, "do you need?"
"Why?" they responded.
"Why what?" asked The Almighty.
"Throughout the planet," they continued,
"Women are abused.
We are bought and sold.
Work our hands and hearts to the bone.
Even in so-called Developed Countries
We are expected to do so much for so little.
We just want to know why."

The Almighty sat back in the rocking chair.
"Fair enough" came the reply.
"I created you so that men
Would see that true strength has nothing to do
With muscle or intimidation
And that sustainable power is given, but never taken.

You are the mirror against which I will judge men.
As they have been seen by you,
So shall they be seen in my presence."

Word of the meeting traveled throughout Heaven.

People of African descent
Were the next to approach
The Council of Archangels.

"What" asked The Almighty, "can I do for you?"
"We have been badly abused.
Our land has been stolen
And the rituals and habits you gave us
Have been dismissed and treated with condescension.
Why did you create us?
What did we do to incur your wrath?"

The Almighty leaned forward to get closer and whispered.
"You did nothing wrong.
I created you so that all would celebrate
The beauty and mastery of my handiwork

I made you as a mirror so the rest of humanity
Would learn their own capacity for kindness or cruelty;
Justice or conquest, honesty or malice.
As they treat you, so shall they be judged."

When Jews heard that women and the children of the Diaspora
Had met with The Almighty
They, too, asked the Council of Archangels
For a meeting.

As they approached, The Almighty smiled
And the Universe came alive with color.
"Yes, my beloveds. What can I do for you?"

"You have chosen us and declared it so
For all to know.
Why then do we have to fight
For every scrap of dignity?
Why are we reviled and cast out time and again?
What value is there to being Chosen?"

(continued...)

View From the Sky Box
(continued)

A soft breeze sighed throughout the Universe.
"Whomever has reviled you when you were humble
Has been brought low" replied The Almighty
"And when you have become proud, arrogant, and cruel
I have taken it all away from you.
You were chosen,
To reflect the power of humility in the world."

"Clearly" turned The Almighty to the Archangels
"It's time to gather everyone together."
So the angels blew their trumpets
And all humanity assembled in response:
All faiths, all nations, all genders, all sizes, all shapes.

As The Almighty lifted the fog of Existence from their eyes,
They could see that the light
Within each other soul
Was just a fragment of the cosmic mirror
Reflecting the soul of The Almighty.

And they understood, finally,
That the Universe is one breath, one light, one spirit
Covered by fleeting illusion.

Grandma Lucy (Dinknesh)

She awoke each morning with the sun,
Fed and prepared her family,
Then did what had to be done
To make a home for another day,
All the while asking
"What's the meaning of my life?"

3.2 million years,
100-thousand generations later
Her bones rose from their rest
To prove that we are
All children of the African dust;
Erasing our differences,
Binding us in our humanity
Together... forever.

Telescope Woman

Her lens pointed at a droplet
She thinks she sees the whole world
And misses the whales
Gliding past her
In an ongoing parade
To refute her hypotheses.
If only she would look up
Turn left or right, up or down.
It's so much easier to know what you see
Than to see what you'll never know.

God's Man

Sunday mornings he pumps hope into the collapsing veins of dispirited souls,
preaching of god's-love-that-he-gave-his-only-begotten,
yet teaching families to throw away the children who love differently than he does,
trading salvation for god's-own-image-just-like-me.

Mondays, he moves among young men at the bus station
asking: Why-are-you-here?-Don't-you-know-god-loves-you?
dismayed by their deadpan unresponsiveness,
as determined to sell them redemption as they are to sell their bodies,

Never seeing the connection
between the love he stole on Sunday
and is trying to replace on Monday.

Amen.

Religious.
Right.

Quietly, whispering,
Evil laughed.
The bet was won,
The door unlocked.

One by one they were torn apart:
Dark skin, light skin,
Blonde hair; black,
Brown eyes, blue eyes.

Man from man from woman from woman
One from one, alone
Judged by their self-chosen hatred
Separated by their self-proclaimed wall of Right-ness.

Doomed to burn in eternal passion for their truth
Driven apart by Fear
Passing poison cell to cell.
Evil reigned.
Love, at last, was vanquished.

Yom Kippur

My heart releases
a waterfall
of tears
Plunging
through fears
Wrenching free
the year's built-up
bile
of anger, hurt, and
disappointment
To be washed down the River
Forgive But Not Forget.

Grace

You drove me deep,
deep down
into the well
'til my pleading eyes
were out of your sight
and the wail of my spirit
beyond your hearing.
You did not know
the walls were made
of gold
and the sweet river
of Life
ran below.

2:00am

Chorus:
Somewhere in the world
A man lies curled in his lover's embrace
Somewhere in the world
A child has wonder playing 'cross her face
And somewhere in this open ocean
we call life
Somewhere in the day/night mists
There's a glimmering shadow
Calling me.
Somewhere.

Verse 1:
Whose whisper do I follow
That keeps me on this search
And urges me toward hope and not despair?
When I am past aloneness
Into the silent dark
What siren-song compels me ever onward?

Verse 2:
Is anybody out there,
Or is this just a dream
A hide-and-seek concoction of my mind?
The yearning that has led me
To the place where I now stand,
Was it your call
Or just an echo of my aching lonely cry?

11

Individuals
Standing side by side
Adding value to each other
Yet having substance alone.

The perfect twosome.

Eternal Life

Michelangelo found it!
The key to eternal life
Is hidden neither in liquid nor metal
It's not consumable or injectable.
What keeps Michelangelo forever alive
More than five centuries later
And brings essential humanity
Pouring out of us,
Who never met him,
Yet honor him nonetheless
And feel consecrated by his gifts to us
Is his soul's manifestation of Love
Through Art,
The only true eternal bequest.

Endings

Endings, in real life,
don't come in big waterfall splashes
They drip, instead,
moment by moment:
a word not spoken
a sigh without pleasure
a gaze unreturned.
And soon the river
has turned to stones
and all that's left is the
pronouncement
of last rights.

Not intended for polite company

Daniel's Song

An instrument
Of gold, or steel, or wood, or tin,
Can only be judged
By the skill of the musician.

I have been strummed
By children
Who only knew I made a pleasant noise
That made their ears tingle.

I have been bowed
By beginners
Who played their basic melodies
And celebrated their victories over me.

But once,
Once I was taken by a Master.

Strong, lean hands led the bow
Through the Melody of Life.
The perfect, rose-sweetness of each note
Blended into our summer's eve song.

My body came alive.
Each stroke took my breath away.
What had been the empty hollow of my being
Vibrated with Life.

I sang.
And I sang his song
Of life.

Now? He's gone.
I can't bear the hands of strangers.
I hear his song and remember
And hunger to play it again.

But...

Children only strum and pick;
Beginners revel in their victories over me;
I... I play a new song, a hungry song.
And, once again, I am hollow.

That Finger
(for Dan)

It traced the fullness of my lips
And brushed the apples of my cheeks.
It circled my erect nipples
And traced the line down my belly
"From the mountains to the valley".

It found the way into my innermost secrets
And drew tune after expert tune from my body
It knew me in the darkest night and brightest day
Pointed out my missteps and showed me the way to go.

How could that finger,
Gentle, warm, hard, smart, funny, sweet
Squeeze metal to metal
Splattering your memories on aluminum and concrete
Reaching out over time and space
To shatter my mirror of love gone by
Leaving a cavernous wound in my soul.

Barbie Dogs

I am a dog with no master
Alone
Proud and hungry
Go where I want
Envied by shampooed, collared pedigrees
Watching me lick my wounds
Through the plate glass of their cosseted lairs
Vicariously reliving my pain
From their blankets in front of the living room fireplace
Knowing only what they're told to know
Turning tricks for kibbles and bits
Unaware of the strength in their own jaws
Or the hidden speed of their haunches
While I roam the world at my own pace
Unafraid.

The Fox

When he was a pup
The fox used his cute little yelps
And big, innocent eyes
To get past the hen house gate
And do… well… what foxes do.

As he grew
And more chicks turned up with broken wings
Or went missing altogether
The hens began to talk
And soon they all knew the Real Deal.

Then one day
The fox came to the gate
And heard the hens chattering away.
"They're excited to see me"
He thought.

You see,
In all the years
Fox had never bothered
To learn hen-talk
So he couldn't know they were laughing.

"That 'ole fool fox is at the gate again"
Said the oldest hen.
"Doesn't he know,"
Asked the youngest chick
"That we all know the Real Deal?"

And so it came to pass
That the fox spent his latter years
Chasing mice and being outrun by rabbits
And never again
Tasted the satisfaction
Of a good chicken dinner.

White Widow Spider

Luring them with
promises of pleasure
Mr. Johnson
firmly between your lips
drawn inward
Until
At their moment of ecstasy
you clench
the incisor
at the back of your velvet
tunnel
Tearing them into digestible bits
Sucking from their death
Your future.

When Bills Come Due

What's that you say, Reverend Bell?
How many women will it take
Until he has traded-up to the top?
Girl Green Stamps
Licked with lies
Held down by unkept promises
Pasted in his book until he has enough
To buy…
What?
Barbie?

Tell your brothah I need more
than an
Apology.
I need change.
Remember
Payback's gender is woman.

Crystal

One teardrop away from a breakdown,
She walked the aisles of Baccarat, Wedgewood and Waterford
Searching for the source of the
        ear-splitting
                shattering
                        splintering
Smash,
Awonder at the calmness of other shoppers.
Until
        she stumbled
Upon the raw-edged fragments of her life.

Who are you?

Containers
Strewn across the timescape of their generation
Chanel, Valium, Dior, Jim Beam
Etched in their foreheads
Ripped from their guts,
Pinned and sprayed to their proper masks
For all to see
And none to know.
Mother, mommy, mom,
Mitera, Madre, Mere, Mamman, Ma.
Lost behind the blessed fog of time
Leaving their daughters a legacy of question marks.

Gold chains

He was found in the middle of the road
This morning just after daybreak
Drowned beneath the torrential floodwaters
Hidden from his misadjusted headlights.

Versace noosed his neck.
Rolex enclosed his wrist
Nikes weighed down his ankles
He was cushioned by Lexus leather.

His wide-eyed grimace
Stared toward the sistah in the corroded Dodge Dart
With whom he shared the knowledge of
Abrupt finality;
His eternal graveside neighbor;
Testifying to his post-mortem understanding
of irony.

The Soloist

Turns out I'm a soloist
Open my songbook
And every tune is written in my key
Arranged to please me
Performed my way

When I tour
The only baggage I carry is my own
The only instrument I tune and polish belongs to me
Those who cannot be responsible for their own load
Those who would overload the orchestra
With their burdens
Are left behind

My performances
Are joyous, unencumbered events
Filled with appreciation for the moment
Built on interlocking notes of human experience
And building the foundation for tomorrow's laughter

Forty-three

Alone I strode through the gates of middle age
Adorned in thorns, reeds, flowers and feathers
Gathered along my journey,
To find this was a black-tie affair.
By invitation only.
Respondez s'il vous plaît.

Remember Time

Remember the days when love
streamed like so much sunshine
it was everywhere you looked
and you couldn't help but get some all over you?

Remember the nights when music
was our heartbeat
keeping us awake, alert, alive
with a sure knowledge it would all be there Forever?

Remember the sunsets
filled with shared sighs, soft laughter,
and tender fingertips
in slow motion until the sun dripped into the sea?

It seemed so easy to live
in wonder, adventure, satisfaction
and feed on expectations, plans
that would come to pass… someday.

Did anyone tell us the hourglass sand
would take so much with it?

Dreamer

Enfolded in a silken home
Kept from wind, ice and rain
Growing silently beneath the tender leaves.

Who prepared you for the glory of your outstretched wings?

Dazzling yellows, reds, blacks
Spread against the verdant meadow
Lush tomato in a sparrow's evening salad.

Mrs. B, It's About Your Son

"He's not like other boys," they say.
"He won't go out to romp and play.
Just wants to mess around with rocks,
Says they have souls inside those blocks."

"What can we do, dear Mrs. B,
When faces in the clouds he sees
And hands reaching from sky and earth
Resulting in our human birth?"

"While teachers talk about Fine Arts
He doodles lots of body parts:
Arms and legs and hands and feet
And some parts very 'incomplete.'"

Yes, that is what they say to me.
Yet I know what my boy will be:
A master craftsman, just you see,
An artist of the first degree.

Like other boys? I sure hope not!
My Michelangelo's best of the lot!

Poetry 101

Poets are souls
damned
to write with the clarity of a mountain spring
what readers
will
inevitably
pollute
with their
own conceptions.

The end

Bitterness is the Cloak
Behind which
Love can die
With Dignity.

www.ingramcontent.com/pod-product-compliance
Lightning Source LLC
Chambersburg PA
CBHW041609220426
43667CB00001B/18